From a

John Spencer

# WARTIME FUN

John Spencer

**BALBOA**.PRESS

A DIVISION OF HAY HOUSE

Balboa Press books may be ordered through booksellers or by contacting:

Balboa Press
A Division of Hay House
1663 Liberty Drive
Bloomington, IN 47403
www.balboapress.com.au
AU TFN: 1 800 844 925 (Toll Free inside Australia)
AU Local: (02) 8310 7086 (+61 2 8310 7086 from outside Australia)

Print information available on the last page.

ISBN: 978-1-9822-9451-9 (sc)
ISBN: 978-1-9822-9452-6 (e)

Balboa Press rev. date: 04/28/2022

# CONTENTS

This little book is dedicated to the parents and teachers who shielded us from the barbaric horrors and atrocities of 80 yeas ago but also to the present guardians who are now repeating this vital humanitarian role for the children of Ukraine.

World war two commenced in 1939 when I was only three years old and it raged on until 1945 when I was nine. Consequently my formative years, as they are sometimes referred to coincided with a state of war, destruction and a struggle for survival with official estimates for casualties being 75 million deaths, 45 million being civilians.

There are countless books, films and documentaries on World war two, representing various aspects, opinions, horrors and the sequelae of what was one of the most destructive and lethal events ever experienced by modern civilization. As a child of the generation who lived through these regressive and barbaric times I was not only unaware of the seriousness and possible consequences but as passive onlookers we were paradoxically entertained and amused by the associated activities of every day life. To a child that lived and survived was exciting! Some of these memories remain lucid whilst others are like palimpsests or images remaining on ancient parchments or neglected notice boards.

December 1940 seems a lifetime ago but despite only being 4 years of age many vivid memories remain.

Instead of being tucked up in my comfy warm bed in the upstairs front bed room of our semi-detached house in suburban Sheffield

I was lying, half sitting uncomfortably in an old folding wooden deck chair in our "Air raid" shelter and although not actually uncomfortable I was aware that the wooden legs were standing in about half an inch of muddy water. A flickering candle standing in an old saucer was the only source of light, casting eerie shadows on the wooden ceiling.

Air raid shelter sounds formal as if built for purpose but in reality it was the space under our kitchen with approximately five feet headroom from floor to ceiling. Some of the clutter such as half bricks, bits of piping and wooden off cuts left by the builders several years previously remained on the floor The ceiling of our "sanctuary "was the wooden beams supporting the kitchen floor boards. Access was through a narrow trap door usually hidden under the doormat with a home made wooden stepladder leading down. There was also a narrow external entrance with a green door leading to the back garden and lawn.

Despite the primitive nature of our shelter we believed we were superior to our neighbours because their under floor space was too low for a shelter so they had a large steel cage under the dining room table called an Anderson shelter into which the family of five (including the elderly grandma) would crawl for safety. Great for playing hide and seek at other times but claustrophobic and very uncomfortable in an air raid, They reassured us that the manufacturer had told them that the shelter was crush proof even if the entire house collapsed on top of it. Fortunately neither our makeshift shelter nor the neighbors steel Anderson sanctuary were put to the test!

The reason for this departure from daily life was of no consequence to me except that I was aware it involved an enemy called Germans who came from overseas and were flying overhead in order to drop bombs on us. Only when I reflect on these memories do I realize the emotional burden and fear the war must have wrought on my parents who were obviously aware of the possible consequences of large bombs raining on the city centre even though we were in the suburbs.

The was no denying these sinister events as intermittently was the booming rumbling of exploding bombs and incendiary devices as they demolished munitions factories, steel works and domestic houses on the east side of the city. I still have a clear memory of my father coming through the external trap door during a lull in the noise; my mother asking him if there was still anything happening to which he replied, "No, just a bit of shrapnel" It was several years later when I discovered that shrapnel were small molten fragments of bombs or shells that sheered off in all directions as they exploded. The next day little boys would look for shrapnel after a raid as it acquired fascinating twisted shapes that one could swap with friends and for while "Shrapnel collecting" and exchange became a hobby.

The Sheffield Blitz (or Blitzkrieg, as the Germans called it) was a carefully planned exercise to destroy the iron steel and munitions factories of Sheffield that were manufacturing equipment like tanks, ammunition, engines, weapons and other vital weapons for the British war effort. The raids, known as the Scheiziegel (to the Germans) were carefully planned and cleverly arranged for the 12th and16[th] December 1940 at a full moon when coincidentally the skies were cloudless and clear. So whilst dozing in my deck chair I was unaware of the horrendous destruction and slaughter occurring just a few miles away.

The damage and carnage was catastrophic. Over 600 people died during these two moonlit evenings of bombing, 1,500 were injured, 30,000 homes were demolished leaving 40,000 homeless. How the emergency services and hospitals of the time coped with these horrendous demands must have been an overwhelming challenge. 20 years later these thoughts would occasionally come to me when as a junior doctor in the Infirmary casualty department I would be mildly irritated when summoned from my bed to work after midnight!

Sheffield's famous theater where the world snooker championships are played is called the Crucible that is the English translation for Scheiziegel. I wonder if this name was an intentional memorial to those tragic events of the Sheffield Blitz?

# THE LEGACY

The aftermath of the Blitz lasted years. Despite the assistance of a full moon and clear skies many bombs missed the intended targets demolishing businesses and properties that were of no strategic consequence but left behind large holes poetically (and predictably) known as" Bomb craters". These were exciting and, fascinating to small boys (most of whom couldn't swim) There were shattered bits of air raid shelters, distorted bicycle frames, wheels, naked dolls and old car bodies and the idea that this glorious post war playground might have been a health hazard was not even an issue.

Miraculously the Cathedral, town hall and the Cutlers hall were all saved from the destructive bombs that had wrought such collateral damage. Some of these remnants remained for months and the stagnant waters became littered with old cans, empty bottles waste paper and the occasional dead cat.

A few of the Luftwaffe bombs failed to explode creating dangerous situations that necessitated the closing of whole segments of the city until the services of bomb disposal experts rendered them safe. One such unexploded specimen had miraculously become lodged under the Wicker arch. As a child shopping down town with my mother these-post Blitz artifacts had became the norm of Sheffield's landscape and shoppers passed them by as part of the down town environment.

Following the devastation and human traumas of the Blitz Sheffield received a formal visit from Winston Churchill. I did not see him personally but was very much aware that he was both special and important as I carefully studied the large photographs on the front page of the Sheffield Telegraph showing him, cigar in one hand and waving his famous V sign in the air with the other. Even though it was only a black and white image the sense of pride that he was in the place where I lived remains imprinted in my memory. A few days later King George and Queen Elizabeth graced the city as they inspected the damaged factories and demolished houses and chatted with locals but the powerful Aura of Churchill is a more dominant memory.

Whilst the significance and seriousness of the war had little impact on me there was one phenomenon that destabilized my passivity and that was the eerie wailing sound of air raid sirens. This penetrating sound commenced softly and insidiously increasing in volume with a sense of urgency and panic urging the population to seek safety from a possible air raid. Even today when I hear a similar siren sound, especially in one of the many war movies my anxiety levels automatically increase to a state of illogical panic.

# RATIONING

Most daily essential requirements were rationed. Bread, clothing milk, toilet paper, sugar, flour, tea etc were all available in quantities carefully calculated by health authorities as being optimal requirements for a family. The system was cleverly calculated and controlled by means of official rationing books so that every time one went to the shops the appropriate coupon was torn out and handed over to the shopkeeper. Children were granted special allowances to ensure they were receiving the appropriate nutritional and essential vitamin requirements. Fruits and vegetables were in short supply, many unavailable entirely and I remember craving for bananas remembering with nostalgia having them sliced up with cornflakes and milk before the war commenced.

# Black Diamonds

*"Keep the home fires burning, whilst your hearts are yearning*
*Though your lads are far away, they dream of home."*
(Popular wartime song)

Just keeping warm in winter was a constant challenge as apart from electricity for lighting and the weekly bath (mine was Wednesday night) that required a half hour boost from the immersion heater, controlled by a switch on the kitchen wall most of our useable energy came from coal. Coal was also the basic commodity necessary for producing carbon monoxide gas for cooking and all towns and cities had "Gas works" and the familiar ugly gasometers necessary for maintaining pressure and storage. Unfortunately I never realised until many years later "that putting one's head "in the gas oven was a euphemism! In fact it was so powerful that we found it an amusing explanation for the disappearance of some one whom we only vaguely knew.

This vital commodity sometimes referred to as "Black diamonds" was kept in a small outhouse known as "t'coil oil," adjacent to the back door. As with all vital consumable commodities coal was rationed to a carefully calculated number of sacks a month. I cannot recall our allowance but I clearly remember my mother counting the one hundred weight sacs as they were carried from the coal lorry at the end of the drive by a couple of very coal dust blackened men. On their backs they wore shiny leather protectors that facilitated both the ease of removal from the truck and the tipping of the precious fuel into the depths of t'coil oil.

Following their departure was the laborious task of sweeping up the inevitable spillage and black dust that remained on the drive and foot path. This was a chore and never an enjoyable duty except when a large shiny black diamond was found on the curbside that had accidentally "fallen off the back of the lorry" Such a large free treasure would keep the old kitchen range burning until bedtime thus ensuring a cosy kitchen for several for hours.

The importance of a good coil Oil became glorified by the once popular Yorkshire song.

> *Reet down int' coil oil, where muck spats on t'winders*
>
> *We've used up alt'coil and we're reet down to cinders.*
>
> *If t'bum baliff comes round*
>
> *Then he'll never find us*
>
> *Cos we're reet down in t'coil oil.*
>
> *Wh'ere muck splats on t'winders*

Of course this song refers to those houses whose "coal holes "were hidden in the cellar.

# PUBLIC HEALTH AND WELFARE

Downtown Sheffield, just off Leopold Street was the central health clinic where one could obtain advice, assistance and new rationing books. The clinic was also the supplier of bottles of delicious concentrated sweetened orange juice affectionately known as "Clinic Orange". This was only supplied on condition the previous weeks empty bottle was returned along with the appropriate coupons. Consequently even as children we were familiar with the system and travelling by an efficient yet noisy, bell clanging tram was just part of daily life.

Because of the war there was universal acceptance of this control of our lives and welfare as essential to survival. Even today health expert's comment that these carefully thought out nutritional regulations were responsible for many positive health statistics such as low levels of obesity, hypertension and cardiovascular disorders. Sadly and predictably the incidence and prevalence of lung cancer due to cigarette smoking was6[th] high – one of the famous victims being King George 6th himself.

The war and it's many restrictions inspired the population to use what my mother called "Initiative". Carl Jung is correct in noting that nothing unites people more than a common aggressor and the war certainly fostered this sense of unity and collective purpose. A similar view is Douglas Adam's theory that there are three distinct sequential phases to all civilizations that he neatly describes as Survival, Enquiry and Sophistication and the war had quickly thrust the nation back into survival mode stimulating most citizens to make some positive contribution.

Thousands of women joined the Land Army taking over the vital work of the men who were now in the armed forces. The Home guard, fire watching, volunteer fire services and ambulance driving were just a few of the contributions made by previously ordinary citizens, many who were women.

Conscientious objectors to fighting were regarded with an element of shame and cowardice and sent to work on farms and agricultural enterprises.

# HEN FOOD

My father, whose early life was in rural Lancashire decided to contribute to the health of the family and built a small chicken coup and pen at the bottom of our small suburban garden. Not only did we have a supply of eggs (and an occasional chicken on special occasions). Our neighbors saved up their kitchen and other food waste that our hens consumed in the special mash we made This mash is one of my less agreeable wartime memories. It was not Cordon bleu even by hen standards!

The family sat on stools or chairs in a circle in the centre of which was a metal bucket into which we would drop in broken up or shredded stale bread, cabbage, peelings and other unidentified scraps (Many from the neighbors.) All done bare handed and I still sense a feeling of tactile and olfactory revulsion as I put these reflections into words even though it is more than 75 years ago!

My father then added some bran meal from a large sack, a spoon full of nameless vitamin liquid and finally a kettle full of hot water. Then he stirred the murky brown pungent contents with the boiler stick until it was thoroughly mixed. At this point we would race to the sink to wash off the sticky remnants on our hand and under fingernails. All this for a few eggs and an occasional chicken!

# NEW BREAD

Thursday (Dads' half day) was baking day. My mother had one of those classical yellow and white bread bowls into which she placed white flour from a sack to which she added special yeast from a small paper packet. This, she insisted was very important because it was "alive" and essential for a successful dough. This I could never understand – how could such a drab looking bit of white of plasticize be alive? Following a measured quantity of cold water she then plunged her hands into the mixture, spending at least five minutes mixing it up until it turned into podgy dough. The bowl and contents were then covered with a tea towel and left on the kitchen table until after lunch by which time it had risen to at least three times the original volume and looked like an obese podgy stomach. Such was my fascination with this metamorphosis that I occasionally lifted the cloth and stuck my finger into the centre creating a doughy umbilicus. Predictably this was not appreciated and caused me considerable strife.

The risen dough was placed into greased bread tins or a separate flat metal cooking tray and put in the coal heated kitchen range oven to bake. After an hour it was removed from the oven and placed on a special tray releasing the mouth watering addictive smell of freshly baked bread. As soon as it had cooled one of the rolls was sliced and a knob of butter smeared on top. This was the wonderful gastronomic climax to many a Thursday!

# GERMAN BREAD – A NIGHTMARE

Whilst I had no concept of who Germans were, why they were a problem to us or who this evil man Hitler was, my unconscious recognized the archetypal enemy as being German. This evil shadow was projected as a recurring nightmare in which a group of men in some unidentifiable uniform broke into the house and stole the freshly baked bread rolls off the kitchen table, carried them out, crossed the road and then with obvious greed, laughter and enjoyment proceeded to eat them all. This was the essence of my hate towards the enemy. No matter what they really wanted they had stolen from my mother, the source of all that a child requires: love, certainty and food. My anger and fury, even though experienced in a dream would sometimes wake me from sleep. If this was what Germans did they should all be exterminated!

# MRS WILCOX

Next door but one up the road lived Mr and Mrs. Wilcocks. He was a specialist in servicing and repairing church organs in the many small village churches in Sheffield and adjacent Peak District. Predictably the back of his Jowett car was usually cluttered with an assortment of fascinating tools and gadgets of his trade.. Consequently he would be away most of the day leaving his chronically disabled wife in bed with no support apart from an ancient bedside telephone. The National Health Service was yet to come. So every Thursday afternoon my altruistic Christian mum would wrap a couple of freshly baked rolls in a clean tea cloth and place them in a straw basket that my brother and I would take round to Mrs Wilcocks back door and reluctantly knock. A thin whiny voice bade us enter and we carried our offering through the cluttered kitchen into the bedroom where the old lady was sitting up in bed with a lace shawl covering her puny shoulders. Her delight at being visited by two shiny faced cherubic little boys and the smell of freshly baked bread was sadly not reciprocated!

She was thin and frail, propped up by multiple pillows and wore special dark glasses with side shades to keep out excess light –not unlike modern worn out swimming goggles. Her hands were gnarled, bent and twisted by years of chronic rheumatoid arthritis.

After telling us how delighted she was to see us she would be plunged into a spasm of rasping, coughing and wheezing, often leaning over the edge of the bed and expectorating a mouth full of green purulent sputum into a bucket already half an in inch deep from previous episodes. These visits were definitely not part of the fun of war and were repressed in my unconscious for years until as a junior medical student on a ward round our consultant Dr Gumpert describing chronic bronchiectasis and bronchorrea evoked a sudden visual flash back to Mrs. Wilcocks miserable predicament and the absence of community medical care during those dark wartime days.

# Free Entertainment

Not only was our generation of children unaware of the serious implications of the war there was intrigue and paradoxically, entertainment to be had. One day across from our front gate a large piece of heavy iron machinery with large metal wheels was trundled down the road by a group of men in military uniform. On top of this contraption was a grey floppy bag with large elephantine ears. As we stood gazing with awe and fascination one of the men turned on a large tap, followed by a loud hissing noise and the bag began to swell up miraculously in front of our eyes. Then a more senior assistant turned a large handle attached to a rusty gear wheel that in turn released some wire hawsers on a large metal drum. Then, like magic the swollen floppy bag changed shape into a shining silver Ariel Jumbo the Elephant that slowly ascended gracefully into the air above our heads. Even the ears flapped as if they were alive!

There were many of these hydrogen filled barrage balloons scattered around the city skies, designed to deter low flying enemy planes with their lethal cargoes. Whether or not they worked we never discovered but they were fascinating first-rate fun and the operators obviously enjoyed their role entertaining the local boys.

My young brother relates an exciting balloon incident involving a Tiger moth biplane that flew above this sea of grey Balloons, presumably overseeing and monitoring their positions and general orderliness. One afternoon as they gazed with fascination at the tiny single engine noisy plane. The pilot who had presumably seen them banked low and waved a large red handkerchief. I understand the ecstasy and sense of jubilation lasted several days and still remains indelible in his memory to this day!

One could purchase bread from Davies store at Bents Green, our local shopping centre. Bents Green seemed (to me) to have everything required for the good life. The local Hardware store (known as the Ironmongers) was dark and dingy but also an Aladdin's cave run by Mr. Goodwin who wore the classical light khaki three quarter length overalls. His shop was full of fascinating gadgets, hardware; garden equipment, spanners, screwdrivers, paint, paintbrushes of all sizes and varieties of household paraphernalia. Just looking at this great variety of stock was a fascinating and free form of entertainment only terminated when Mr. Goodwin asked us to leave as his premises were not a venue of free entertainment for little boys. The row of shops also included the fruit and vegetable shop run by Mrs. Turner, an obese woman with a loud scary voice who disliked little boys. Next was Davies the Bakers and bread shop that suffered from the constant smell of the adjacent wet fish shop that sometimes had large crabs from Filey lying on their backs, claws and pincers in the air creating a menacing spectacle to young children gazing with curiosity and apprehension. The end establishment was the stationers and post office run by a humorless couple with the unfortunate and amusing names (to young boys) of Crapper and Waite.

Bents Green was a fifteen minutes walk from home and as the eldest (now about eight) my twice-weekly duty was to collect two unsliced loaves from Davies, the bread shop. So in possession of an extendable, string bag, four pence halfpenny and the essential bread coupons in my jacket pocket I would dutifully make the journey.

What could have become a tedious repetitive ritual was never an issue as the walk passed the Grammar school playing fields that had been converted into a fascinating military establishment. On the previously immaculate cricket pitch was a large gun, the gleaming menacing barrel directed heavenwards.

Sometimes soldiers were practicing, turning large wheels and pulling levers causing it to either rotate or change the angle of the large barrel. As they maneuvered this lethal monster I fanaticized enormous shells zooming upwards and totally annihilating a large German bomber and watching as a ball of flames came crashing down to the waste grounds we called the Roughs. All this was real life – not comics, or the local Cinema screen and no one yet possessed the luxury of a television.

Peering through the iron railings one could see the giant searchlight on it's rotating axis glinting in the sunshine, being polished earnestly by a couple of young men in grey overalls. This I realized was the origin of the brilliant finger of light we sometimes saw scanning the night skies as we gazed upward from my Dads rose garden.

Further on in a treeless corner of the field was a strange, mysterious contraption resembling an enormous twenty-foot tall metal and wire four sided clothes drier, slowly, almost deliberately rotating through 360 degrees. Peering curiously at this weird contraption, my face pressed at the gap between the railings an elderly man interrupted my thoughts and without formal introduction informed me in a loud voice, "That's called Radar, Lad! it can pick up enemy planes in t'sky even if they are miles away" I was mystified how such an odd almost random arrangement of wires and cogwheels could possibly know what was in the sky miles away. He was quite correct as it turned out but it was a total mystery to me just how it worked. "Even when it's cloudy" he said before continuing his way to Bents Green.

# Evacuees

Sheffield was one of several cities that experienced aerial bombardment from the Luftwaffe and it's fleets of Dornier's, Henkel's and Junkers. Ports, radio stations Airfields, bridges were all targets over several years resulting in thousands of deaths, injuries and destruction of factories, property, railways and shipping. Consequently millions of people became homeless creating an unprecedented Evacuation system in that people from affected areas would be relocated to more fortunate regions of the country that had not been targeted. This was a major humanitarian exercise and people and families who had never met before arrived at the front door with a couple of suit cases and some carrier bags announcing that they had been selected to come and share our residence as their house in Coventry had been demolished. So, my brother and I moved into the small front bedroom in bunk beds

Our unfortunate evacuees were a young couple, called Facer with a small boy and as far as I can recall we seemed to coexist without any conflict. It has always seemed paradoxical that we were selected as Coventry, also an industrial city was severely damaged by the Germans but to send evacuees to Sheffield did not seem the wisest choice in the circumstances!

Because the population was under the constant sinister shadow of invasion, bombing and a shortage of basic supplies a sense of unquestioned altruism and concern for the welfare of others was apparent. Even as a small boy I was aware of this almost universal phenomenon clearly and recall that one damp grey day a worn out woman in an old grey coat knocked on our front door and asked my mother if she could have a bath. The immersion heater was turned on and while the water heated up my mother provided tea, bread and jam and no doubt listened to her unfortunate story. Whilst I cannot recall the details with clarity when the woman had finally departed the bath was filled with water to which was added a large dollop of strong ammonia presumably to eliminate any unwanted microorganisms left behind.

# PRISONERS OF WAR

Although not evacuees in the conventional sense thousands of Germans were in residence in a purpose built "prisoner of war" camp beyond Lodge Moor estate. The residents were predominantly Pilots, gunners and crews of enemy planes who had parachuted to safety after they had been shot out of the skies when on one of the many air raids. One Saturday afternoon whilst on a bike ride with friends we pedaled over the moors from Ringjnglow Village where to our surprise found ourselves on a ridge a few hundred yards above the camp. Gazing down were hundreds of concrete and wood single story buildings and Nissan huts spread out neatly in almost endless rows. In the centre was an open Quadrangle where several men were noisily playing soccer and shouting excitedly in German. Around the periphery more men were ambling, chatting, laughing and smoking. What a surprise!

The residents were quite different to how I had previously imagined Germans; they looked like normal people – surely these ordinary looking men would never purposefully break into our kitchen and steal my mother's bread or bomb our houses!

Lodge Moor Camp was one of Britain's largest prisons of war camps. Built during the First World War it initially housed Italians but later augmented to house the large number of German Prisoners during world war two.

Situated over a thousand feet high on the edge of the city, the camp was not built for comfort, some describing it as "squalid" and it is estimated that at one time there were eleven thousand residents. Built on the bleak moors on the east side of the city it would have been a test of resilience especially in the middle of winter! Unlike the strict, sometimes punitive camps in Germany the prisoners were treated civilly and as humanely as possible and during the latter stages of the war many were allowed limited time to wander in the neighborhood. Some even participated in local sporting activities such as soccer and my brother and I were quite perplexed when one Saturday afternoon two Germans walked passed our house and bidding us a friendly greeting in a strange foreign language.

After the war there was a serious outbreak of smallpox in South Yorkshire so the facilities were temporally used as an emergency overspill for Lodge moor isolation hospital.

Years later, long after the war on a fine summers afternoon, I stood on the same moorland ridge. All the buildings had disappeared revealing hundreds of crumbling concrete foundations. Weeds had grown where the quadrangle had been and the skeleton of the old watch tower stood defiantly at the entrance on Red mires Road. A couple of years ago all that remained were hundreds of self seeded trees, brambles and bushes hiding the crumbling foundations of what was once Britain's largest prisoner of war camp and temporary residence to eleven thousands young Italian and German prisoners.

Currently the site is of historical interest and has become the focus of local archeologists from Sheffield University who will no doubt produce a comprehensive history of its beginnings, many sad stories and untold secrets. The old concrete alleys are also a favorite practice ground for learner drivers.

# Involuntary Prisoners of War

Paradoxically our parents were also prisoners. Prisoners of the restrictions, regulations and the stringent rationing of life's essentials. However I never heard complaints and the concept of human rights or infringement of will was still a debate for the future generation.

My father was not a philosophical man and accepted the rules of life without question; perhaps he was grateful that the system exempted him from "joining up" because as a pharmacist his civil role was deemed more important than being a soldier. As a boy he was a compliant child, never questioning the harsh parental rules of inflexible rural Lancashire parenting and much of his language revealed this austere inflexibility. The attic was the "Cock loft" and if someone were in his way, he would shout "Let the dog see the rabbit! An utterance that requires no further explanation!

As a parent he was a kindly, at times quite jocular man, unphilosophical and of simple faith attending church every Sunday for "evensong" which was a trial of patience for my brother and me. His sanctuary was his garden where he excelled in growing aromatic tomatoes (pollinated in the spring by a fluffy rabbits tail on a small stick,) chrysanthemums and lettuce – much of which was given to neighbors. In addition to these interests he was also a competent amateur photographer and very proud of his ancient Rollieflex (Still in one of our old cupboards).

As a chemist he trained at the London School of pharmacy before becoming an apprentice for four years at a pharmacy called "Thornbers" where he worked for a pittance before finally being allowed to dispense (usually from prescriptions written in indecipherable Latin script). He never drank alcohol or visited pubs: the fashion had not started but he smoked ten cigarettes daily – his silver initialed cigarette case still sitting in our display cabinet. Apart from a universally shared opinion of Hitler he had a serious critical dislike of Masons!

My mother was also of rural Lancashire stock and was the youngest child of four of a simple church going Christian family, her father being a member of the church committee. My mother known to all, as Mary was an excellent cook, having trained at Elizabeth Gasgill College near Manchester and we all recognized her talents (I still have her recipe for rabbit pie). I cannot remember her ever loosing her temper but she had store of apposite moral quotes that she would deliver on occasions. One that troubled me was, "John, remember your sins will eventually find you out!" How the hell did she know? And was she right? Unlike my father she had no hobbies apart from knitting – a pastime that I found fascinating and for a while I attempted to copy by making dishcloths on large wooden needles.

Being "refugees" from rural Lancashire most of my parent's friends were neighbors or associates of the local church, my mother being a stalwart of the fellowship of marriage. I understand the focus of this group was centered on what was called Parish Room tea and current scones and the occasional prayer.

# War Time School

It was with considerable apprehension that I experienced my first day at school.

I walked along the gennel with a friend who sadly I no longer remember. Over one shoulder I carried a leather school satchel. On the other was a grey canvas bag containing my gas mask, the latter smelling of the fresh rubbery odor of the facemask above, which was the cellophane window to view the outside world! The entire contraption fastened on to ones head with two straps that fastened neatly with two buckles.

So, complete with new trousers, a white shirt and tie, knee length socks (held up with elastic garters) and polished shoes I arrived at the playground where scores of boys were playing impromptu soccer. A large boy seeing me arrive asked if I wanted to kick up or down the inclined asphalt yard. Without hesitation I opted for down. "Ret', he said," That's Sheffield United, put yer bags in't corner and join in". This impulsive emotive decision, made nearly eighty years ago has never been questioned and wherever I travel in the world I am compelled to check the latest result and their current position in the league table.

The school playground was an important area for us all for in addition to the football activities others would congregate in small groups to talk (and shout) about local affairs, a father on leave from the army or about a tank that had driven down the road.

One little boy, believing himself to be a Sheffield tram would spend his play time trotting round the periphery of the yard shouting," clang, clang" (as the trams did) when some other boy got in his way, simultaneously turning the handle on the fantasy control panel. Only in retrospect do I now realise that he was afflicted by the then unrecognized and undiagnosed Aspergers disorder.

At the bottom of the yard was a primitive urinal emitting the curious odor of a blend of urine and Izal Germicide? On the wall was a chalk line indicating the current record for high pee-ing – usually by an infamous lad called Michael Grundy. Next-door was the residence of Mr. and Mrs. Derbies house, the school janitors. They were well known by the boys for the buckets of sand they always had ready to pour on to vomit that occasionally appeared on the playground.

Sadly I was only "kicking down t'yard" for a few minutes when a shrill whistle brought all to a sudden halt. This sudden intrusion interrupting the vital game was not an invisible referee but Mrs. Booth the J. four teacher who was renowned for her love of order and strict discipline. Within seconds all the young soccer players were lined up in twos, military style by the school entrance waving her finger from side to side, "Left, Right, Left, Right!" Then, like a mini- battalion of junior soldiers we marched in strict order to our various classrooms to join the girls who had entered from their separate playground.

This regimentation of school children sounds incongruous today but in 1942 it mirrored the everyday scenes of service personnel in the streets and parks of the city, Union jacks flew from many buildings, patriotic notices were a common site urging people to join a variety of voluntary services, fire watching or the women's land army. Every day there would a military marching band followed by a group of enthusiastic lads pretending to be soldiers usually accompany a military parade at Somme Barracks on West Street. So it was predictable that school children would be infected by these collective patriotic sentiments.

The children's art and paintings expressed collective grandiose fantasies about the war and the evil natured Germans. The boys (sometimes encouraged by male teachers) would frequently paint lurid scenes of giant planes, swastika and black crosses on their fuselages plunging to earth in balls of fire whilst in the corner would be a jubilant pilot waving from the cockpit of his shining Spitfire.

I remember a short essay I wrote on the topic of "What I want to do when I grow up". After discarding the idea of being a train driver, decided on the equally popular Airline fighter pilot fantasy. This was apparently regarded above the usual standard and I was asked to read it out as an example of the" importance of "Conclusion" in an essay to the class below. The essay described the challenges and excitement involved in being a pilot and finished with the sentiment, "And if there were any German airplanes left I would shoot them down!"

# Our Very Own Bomb

What is a bomb? How does one make one and why do they make such a noise when they explode and why do they sometimes not explode? For several weeks these questions played on our young curious minds as an unexploded one turned up in the local farmers field until one day we shared our thoughts with one of those precocious older boys called Donald Soppit who lived across the road from David Newsome, one of my best friends. Soppit told us that the simplest easily obtainable explosive was Ammonium nitrite that in 1943 was the basic ingredient in garden weed killer, available in most gardening shops.

So one sunny afternoon we decided to make our own bomb.

David found a large recently sawn log and using his dads electric drill bored a wide six-inch deep hole in the centre of which he placed some old fashioned doubled up fuse wire. Then he carefully spooned in a couple of the innocuous looking weed killer and a small quantity of yellow sulphur powder that he bought at the local chemist. He seemed to know what he was doing as he said," he'd looked it up." Finally he placed a small used cork to seal the hole leaving the two bare fuse wires sticking out of the top. Finally he attached his dad's electric lawn more cable to the two bare wires making sure they were tightly twisted on. The bomb was now snuggly hidden under three large rockery stones unaware and oblivious of their immediate future. Neither were we!

A D.I.Y cable with an On/off switch on the board had been passed through the kitchen window to where we cowered behind a large iron wheel borrow awaiting the excitement. Who was going to press the switch? This was decided by sharing the deed! One would do the talk down (3, 2 .1.Zero! leaving the other the simple task of pressing the ON switch. This procedure seemed so simple and almost, "too easy" Is this how the Germans did it? Somehow they must have some form of remote control systems without needing wires, lawn mower cables or old iron wheelbarrows. These thoughts were only transitory as less than a second later the switch was activated and ear-shattering explosion occurred that was followed by a storm of miscellaneous objects raining down. Pieces of rock. Lumps of soil, the roots of previously healthy rockery plants, a dead mouse were dropping out of the air. A large stone landed noisily on the side of the wheelbarrow scaring us to bits. After less than a couple of minutes it was all over apart from a faint smell of burned ammonia and a grey haze over David's Dads previously neat and tidy garden now looking as if, "A bomb had hit it; as indeed it had! I dread to think what David's father must have thought when later he came home from work. Fortunately I never saw David again for several months and then the "Bomb" was never discussed.

As I was cycling away on that explosive afternoon Donald Soppit who we had not discussed our plans came running across the road to inform us that his front bedroom room windows had cracked due to a mysterious explosion up the road.

I never wanted another bomb.

(David was eventually expelled from school for producing trimethylamine in the school chemistry laboratory after hours

# HAZARDS OF SCHOOL
# WAR SAVINGS

War is a very expensive enterprise. In addition to the massive costs of the vast quantities of military equipment, home defenses, guns, bombs. Shells and vital funding to maintain the health and welfare of the Nation.

Consequently the government devised special saving schemes enabling citizens to contribute to the war effort. Government Bonds with attractive interest rates were introduced with the promise of re-imbursement after the war. One popular scheme was the School War savings scheme. Children were supplied with a Savings book into which pretty stamps worth 6d or a shilling could be licked and stuck into little squares on the pages.

Every Tuesday morning a small table was erected at the front of the infant class room and children queued in orderly alphabetical order awaiting their turn to make their contribution to the teacher who would add the sixpence or shilling to the appropriate neat little piles and tick off the child's name in a little book This day my Mother had given me a shilling which I had thrust deeply into the safety of my pocket for the weekly contribution. As I shuffled up to the table holding the savings book in the left hand I felt for the shilling but apart from an old toffee paper and a dirty handkerchief there was no coin. Then I must have lost my presence of mind as I placed the savings book on the table and flicked the neat pile of shillings over! As they fell into random disorder I shouted out in a squeaky voice," shilling!"

The consequences were predictable. Mr Jenkinson the headmaster was called for and arrived in less than a minute. "John Spencer, did you or did you not put a shilling on the table?" At that moment I was overcome with a sudden urge to wet my pants but managed to contain my self as I timorously lied, "Yes sir". However I new the game was over as Mr. Jenkinson delved into my grubby pocket and there hiding under the scruffy handkerchief nestling in the angled corner he located the shiny coin my mother had given me three hours previously.

This episode lives on forever in my mind! Was it a genuine mistake or as some accused me, was I trying to save a shilling for Jelly babies or Humbugs? Eighty years later I still do not know the answer only remembering the humiliation of being publically searched in front of the entire infants 1 and 2 classes! The incident has also become a longstanding family joke and when ever it was discussed my mother would delight in uttering her favorite moral message to me, "John, Don't' forget your sins will eventually find you out."

Mr. Jenkinson was a strict yet kindly man who we all respected. He was always dressed in a dark suit with matching waistcoat, tie and pocket watch. There was insufficient space for a private office so his desk and chair were on a raised platform at the rear of the junior's one classroom. In addition to the files and papers on his desk there was a telephone and a large handbell, which he rang at break, playtime, lunch and end of the day and prayers.

Mr Jenkinson's brother was a dentist who wisely emigrated to New Zealand before the war where he must have run a successful practice and periodically sent large food parcels and tinned fruit directly to the school.

Mr Jenkinson opened these on his already overcrowded desk and distributed the contents to those families that he believed had the greatest need. There was no shortage of them. Somehow we all recognized the wisdom of his choice.

# Wartime Health And Safety

Schools were ideal venues for public health screening, nutrition and health and safety monitoring. Once a week there was Gas mask practice when all the children would remove the rubber and cellophane monster from it's canvas case, put it on to their cherubic faces and attempt to fasten the straps at the back of their heads – a task usually requiring assistance from Miss Goodfellow, the infants one teacher. The site of over thirty small children sitting with gas mask covering there innocent faces is a macabre memory that today one would expect to see in a futuristic Science fiction horror movie!

Occasionally the school nurse would visit and selected children were examined for ring worm and Nits – the latter involving the use of a special comb that she used on the unwashed heads of those that were referred to as the "Poor Children", a euphemism for the hard up and unwashed and sometimes odorous.

Because school was compulsory it was a convenient opportunity for maintaining basic nutrition requirements. This was effected by what was called the "School Milk" program. Every day, rain or shine a small Morris minor Van delivered several crates of milk containing over a hundred third of a pint bottles. At eleven o clock exactly there was a ten minute break from lessons as we removed the silver tops and with a paper straw greedily consumed the contents. Occasionally on a cold winters day the bottles had to be placed on the hot water pipes for twenty minutes to melt the frozen semi – icy contents.

# WITH GOD ON OUR SIDE

Whenever communities are threatened by disasters, death, famine or war there is a resurgence of religious sentiment. Whenever there are deaths following a natural disaster or a terrorism event those in power usually tell the survivors "They are in their thoughts and prayers" Nice words but I wonder how many of them ever pray to any sort of deity at all. As the war progressed congregation numbers increased, inspired by the belief that somehow God would in some way be on our side and not just protect us but swing victory in our favour because "He was on our side."

People who never gave much thought to religion, God and prayer were precipitated by fear into seeking help from the almighty; who perhaps exists after all! Hence numerous people who had never been inside a church since christening or a wedding decided that perhaps the clergy, assisted by biblical texts and sermons might offer some reassuring answers.

Several questions suddenly arose. In war does God take sides? Is God always on the side of the righteous? Does He still love the enemy even if they are in the wrong? As Christians praying for ourselves should we also be praying for the innocent citizens of the enemy? These old questions are endless but there was an expectation that the vicar in the pulpit should have some reassuring answers and could find these answers from the wisdom of the ancient scriptures as they contains descriptions of scores of wars, massacres and Gods' involvement over the centuries.

As children there was much less ambiguity in answering these philosophical dilemmas. The Germans were bad, Hitler was evil and there was no doubting that God was on our side. Our teachers irrespective of their personal thoughts reinforced this reassuring view. Our little school was a Church school so there was no questioning the fundamental tenets of Christianity. The school day started, all standing, eyes closed, tightly, hands clasped together as we parroted what Jesus apparently taught us 2000 years ago!

> *Our father that art in heaven*
>
> *Hallowed be thy name*
>
> *Thy kingdom come*
>
> *Your will be done on earth as it is in heaven*
>
> *Give us this day our daily bread*
>
> *And forgive us our trespasses*
>
> *As we forgive them that trespass against us.*
>
> *And deliver us from evil*
>
> *For thy names sake.*
>
> *Amen*

Trespass was just another word for sin (we were told) and in our young minds there was no doubting that Hitler and the Germans were on the side of evil from which the Good Lord would deliver us.

Following this ritual, lessons began in the usual manner and following a half hour lunch brake would continue through until three thirty when reminded by Mr Jenkinsons' bell the pious teacher stood in front of the class and with her eyes tightly closed uttered the single word, "Lighten." Hypnotically provoking the entire class, now standing and with eyes also closed tightly would as one voice continue with-

> *"Lighten our darkness O Lord,*
>
> *And by thy great mercy*
>
> *Protect us from the dangers and perils of this night."*
>
> *Amen*

It was never clear to us just what these dangers and perils were but I suspect our teachers probably had constant realistic fears of nocturnal enemy planes bombs, and other frightening imagery.

Being a church school most other activities were associated with the Christian influence. Cubs, Brownies, Scouts Guides and Sunday school activities were under the all-encompassing shadow of the church and involved God, prayers and Jesus in some form. It was mandatory that the curate should be involved in all scouting and guiding activities irrespective of whether he wanted to be or not!

The scouting and guiding movement was a powerful influence on many of us containing a curious blend of religious values, patriotism and a simple morality and with few exception we were indoctrinated with the Boy scout motto as laid down by our unquestioned world leader, Lord Baden Powell

> *I promise to do my duty to God and the King.*
>
> *To obey the scout law.*
>
> *And do a good turn for someone every day.*

Somewhere in Baden - Powell's "Scouting for Boys was the directive that a Boy Scout should "smile and whistle under all circumstances" Easier said than done! The Boy Scout movement was started by Baden Powell to encourage young people to survive in the great out doors, to be patriotic and to look after those who were less fortunate than our selves. At the semi formal initiation ceremony the new recruit would recite the "Scout Law" in front of the whole troop-

1. Promise do my duty to God and the King
2. To obey the Scout law
3. To do a good turn for some one every day

This simple behavioral morality reflects the personality and the ethos of the colonial system at the time but I suspect would not be so enthusiastically accepted by be the liberated pleasure seeking youth of today. Although Baden Powel never expected boy scouts and girl guides' to adopt a military style. This was obvious as whenever we went out on church parade, the local church fete or setting off on a jamboree we were always "In step" and very sensitive to commands such as "Troop Halt, by the left foot quick march Stand at ease, right wheel, left wheel"

The second routine that most of us enjoyed was called "Flag brake". in this ceremony a tightly rolled union Jack was hauled to the top of the flag pole where it rested as a small parcel until we all sang the national anthem before a chosen boy would jerk the second string releasing a cunningly tied slip knot permitting the flag to unfurl and release a collective sensation of patriotism and the command to stand "At ease" One can clearly understand how in these days of multiple distractions and commercial entertainment boy scouts and girl guides have virtually faded into obsolescence. In fact the previous sombre ceremony of standing erect in front of the leaders, saluting with the three fingers of the right hand was hi-jacked by Benny Hill who incorporated it into several of his irreverent and hilarious routines.

Easter, Whitsuntide and Christmas were all celebrated formally with most of the children wearing their best clothes to church and after selected hymns the vicar would address us all and deliver the appropriate seasonal message.

When the war ended in1945 there was a short period of thanksgiving to God for delivering the nation from the evil forces of Hitler and his grandiose beliefs.

Since this time Church of England congregations have consistently dwindled and according to official statistics approximately only 7.5% of the population is now regular attendees.

As a small boy I stood, bored to tears but still clearly remember the underlying meaning in what seems the epitome of the populations request to the almighty for assistance in those troubled times from the last verse of the hymn," Eternal father strong to save" and my father would some times have real tears of emotion as he sang the last few lines.

> *O Trinity of love and power*
>
> *Our brother's shield in dangers hour,*
>
> *From rock and tempest and fire and foe.*
>
> *Protect them where 'ere they go*
>
> *Thus ever more they shall rise*
>
> *To the glad praise from land and air and sea*

# Ration Books And
# The Curious Tale of
# Mr. Brain's Trousers

In 1940 the population of the United Kingdom was approximately 50 million. More than 80 % of the nations fruit was imported from various friendly countries and most meat, cereal, sugar and other vital foods came from overseas and a mysterious place called the colonies.

This vital supply line to the nation was an obvious target for the Germans causing a serious threat to the health and welfare of the population.

To combat this threat the Government created the Ministry of food to regulate and control the supply of food and other threatened substances such as clothing, soap, fuel, paper, butter, bread, sugar and luxury items such as sweets, chocolate and nylon stockings. To deal with this emergency all citizens were issued with Ration books containing coupons. These could be exchanged for the commodities in short supply at Specific shops previously chosen by the customer. Initially there were 66 coupons a year but this varied according to supply and demand.

This was a successful system generally accepted by the people as being necessary for survival. In fact the shortage of vital supplies stimulated a movement of innovation, creativity and predictably back market dealings for cigarettes, Alcohol and nylon stockings.

A culture of "make do and mend" evolved and worn out clothing for instance was repaired, darned or rehabilitated. Cobblers enjoyed a new lease of life soling and healing old shoes whilst the more enterprising hammered Philips "hammer ons" using a cast iron Last – many of which remain today as antique door stoppers. Old blankets were made into warm (if not elegant) overcoats. There was a surge in knitting; repairing and fixing things that in peacetime would have been thrown in the bin. During these difficult times of survival there evolved a collective challenge uniting the community creating a sense of purpose and meaning. There is an extensive literature on these dynamics but it is of interest that during these challenging times suicide rates dropped significantly and the prevalence of obesity was lower than in the relative affluence and abundance of peace time.

The scarcity of clothes was a serious drain on coupons, testing the ingenuity of families especially with growing children. Nylon stockings were almost impossible to obtain but many women improvised by using a special dye painted on the legs. These also included a special pencil that when drawn on the legs effectually simulated seams of the genuine object.

Other enterprising people with experience in tailoring set up home workshops, where with the aid of a sewing machine and patterns one could (at a price) obtain professionally made trousers, jackets or waistcoats.

My father was informed by a work colleague that a certain Mr. Brain was an excellent Taylor, specializing in boys short trousers outfits and thought this could be a solution for my brother and me whose trousers were becoming too small and wearing out at the seat! It would also save on scarce clothing coupons. So, one Saturday afternoon Mr. Brain, a diminutive little grey haired man smelling of stale tobacco carefully measured us using a long white tape measure, chalk, big safety pins, tissue paper and large scissors. "Should be ready in a fortnight", he said as my Dad handed over a crisp five-pound note.

A couple of weeks later we telephoned Mr. Brain whose wife told us that they were not "quite" ready and we should call back in another week. Sadly a week later there was no response to our call. So we phoned the operator, an important person in the days before computers and digital, systems who told us in a strong Sheffield accent the phone was "unattended." For several years whenever we drove up Greystones Road and passed Mr. Brains' house we mourned the loss of the trousers (and the five pounds!) that never materialized. This mystery was never resolved and it was obvious to us that he did not wish to discuss the matter and it remained a shadowy mystery to the day he died.

Due to the constant fear of air raids all windows had to be fitted with "Black out" cloth to prevent light from identifying residential areas and the minority of citizens who owned cars had to have special attachments directing light beams. downwards. Some cars had a large floppy gasbag strapped to the roof replacing the need for scarce and very expensive petrol. Just how these worked remains a mystery to but I clearly remember seeing an old Humber lumbering past the Midland station with such a black canvas bag fastened onto the roof with ropes.

# BUSES, TRAMS AND SMOKING MONKEYS

Whilst only a few "Better Off" people had motor cars and most were Austin's, Morrises, Fords or the occasional Jowett. Some young men had noisy motor bikes such as BSA's, AJS's or Nortons that belched out pungent oily smoke as they roared around the neighborhood; a smell that even today still evokes an ancient nostalgia of these classical machines many of which are now much sought after collectors items.

On the opposite side of our road was a young man who kept his motorbike behind two large green wooden doors and went to work whatever the weather every morning. On some occasions the staccato noise of the engine would backfire loudly alarming the elderly neighbors. My brother and I were fascinated by this daily explosive cacophony and watched with awe and fascination as man and noisy machine secretly wishing we could be a pillion passenger for just a few minutes. There was also a bizarre ritual that developed in the form of shouting out loudly the word "Sausage" as he roared by and then bobbing down below the window level and hiding just in case he might have seen or heard us that in reality would have been physically impossible. Even today when a noisy motorbike goes by I sometimes have to consciously refrain from bellowing out Sausage.

Because only a few people had personal transport most relied on Sheffield corporation buses and trams. The buses were large robust double decker petrol vehicles with the entrance being at the back where steep metal stairs led to the more popular upstairs deck where no one was allowed to stand or spit.

Both trams and buses had a driver and a conductress – the latter usually a bossy controlling woman who was responsible colleting the fares and maintaining an attitude of "good Manners" and discipline in misbehaving boys.

One conductress, well known for her disciplinarian attitude insisted in preventing more than the legal number of passengers from boarding. This she did by the use of a chain that she drew across the entrance thus blocking entry. On one memorable occasion the next in line was a smart, imperious elderly Jewish man carrying a shiny brief case and was consequently denied entry despite pleading that he was the rabbi and had to attend an important meeting at the downtown Synagogue and should be exempted from the official transport departments ruling. Unfortunately his plea for special status was rebutted by the conductresses authoritarian response, "I don't' care if you're Poppie, You're not getting on this bus!"

Trams were much more fun. They were noisy, exiting and one could jump on and off (unofficially) at will. There was less discipline and they tended to rock about on bends and in a way ruled the road as other traffic had to avoid them as their direction was fixed by tram lines in the roads. The driver did not need to steer as the trams trajectory was already determined and all the driver seemed to do was pull and manipulate a couple of crude levers and ring a loud bell by stamping his foot on the cab floor if any one got in the way. As trams could not turn round when they reached the terminus the driver jumped off and wielding a large pole would disconnect the trams electrical connecting rod from the above high power wires, turn it around, reconnect it in the opposite direction and then walk to the other end of the tram for the return journey. These complex (or so we thought) maneuvers were highly entertaining to little boys. Meanwhile the conductor (usually a woman) would walk the length of the tram reversing the direction of the seats. This was a noisy procedure; some conductors would permit the same little boys to assist.

# Mr Macdonalds Monkey

Trams were somehow stable, child friendly and predictable so I was sometimes be trusted to take my younger brother to town to collect the weekly clinic orange juice and ration books. Occsionally it was my task to escort my younger brother to Mr McDonald, the down town barber. Fortunately the tram stop was outside Redgates, the toy and bike shop whilst upstairs was the barbers. Mr McDonalds shop was not what one would ever call a salon as it was originally a Victorian style kitchen with a single barbers chair facing the old kitchen range (Long since removed) above which was a mantle piece on which were an assortment of scissors, razors, combs, clippers, jars of hair cream and other mysterious tools of his trade. Attached to the wall hung a leather strap used for sharpening his cut throat razors. My brother was clearly frightened of having his hair cut and viewed all this equipment with a palpable degree of apprehension.

However Mr Mc Donald was a kindly elderly man, who familiar with little boys fears for which he had developed a novel strategy.

In the centre of the mantelpiece stood a grinning model monkey that looked directly at the customer sitting in the barber's chair. As soon as Bob (my brother was hoisted up into the chair Mr McDonald lit a cigarette and placed it between the pursed lips of the smiling monkey. Completely distracted by the whispy blue smoke ascending towards the ceiling the scissors, clippers and comb were almost unnoticed by my brother and long before the monkeys "Craven A" had burned to a stub the short back and sides was complete. Within minutes we were out of the shop, through Redgates, back on the clanging tram back home to the delight of our mothers sartorial satisfaction.

# PLEASE MAY I HAVE A BATH?

Late one morning on a cold October day a shabbily dressed middle aged woman knocked on our front door. She wore an old grey coat with a turned up collar and a blue berry on her head. Even now I remember the sad face, slouched posture and overall image of misery and despair as she stood on the threshold of our unheated semi-detached residence. After a few second silence she spoke with averted eyes and a mask of shame and asked, "please could I have a bath?" My mother, who by now was hardened and desensitised by the daily consequences of war looked briefly at the sad woman and said, "Come in, I'll turn the heater on; we'll have a cup of tea whilst we wait for it to warm up" The cup of tea expanded and became freshly baked bread with butter and Co-op strawberry jam finished off with a large piece of home made Parkin.

During the course of conversation we learned that the woman's house was one of the 30,000 that had been demolished by the German air raid blitz on the night of 14th December; a week before Christmas, and had since been living in a charitable neighbours cellar since these horrendous events. At the time, her husband was serving in the navy but had died a few months later when his destroyer was torpedoed by a German submarine.

My personal memory ceases at this point in time as I disappeared into the late afternoon light to play street cricket with my usual group of friends. However later in the day when it was becoming too dark for street games I went to the small bathroom/toilet and noticed the strong smell of ammonia emanating from the bath which was three quarters full of cold water that my mother informed me was just to make sure that "no germs" had been left behind.

This tragic event remains in my memory as a cogent reminder that even though most of my childish war memories were associated with fun, laughter and childish enjoyment the memory of this sad, miserable, grieving woman knocking on our front door asking if she could use our bath is engraved indelibly in my mind reminding me that it was not all fun.

# THE LITTLE WHEEL

Our suburb was on the Derbyshire side of the city and one could be in pleasant green farming and rural country on a bicycle in less than half an hour so the city itself was not a primary target for the Luftwaffe but despite this there were a few solitary craters on the peaty moors where retreating bombers simply dropped their unused loads randomly irrespective of what or who may have been a thousand feet below.

Ecclesall was also fortunate in that several years before the war water, electricity and coal gas were connected to most properties and I remember clearly in 1946 when several residents in the village of Ringing low objected to reading by electric light believing it was bad for the eyes when compared to gas mantles.

So, compared to other districts we were fortunate. However when the war descended upon us the price of these utilities increased drastically automatically converting them to luxuries for the average householder. Children, used to having regular baths, electric blankets, electric fires and kettles were suddenly subjected to stringent rationing, time tabling, sharing bath water and boiling the kettle on the coal fired open range. Predictably these restrictions caused considerable stress and grumbling inducing my father to become an unofficial defacto energy inspector checking unnecessary lights, the immersion heater or my mothers electric iron. Eventually he developed a special set of phrases, a sort of code that whilst removing criticism and blame from a particular offender accurately conveyed the nature of the wasting electricity, be it a an unnecessary light bulb or a small one bar electric fire.

The most frequent meaningful emotionally loaded none directional accusative utterance that we all understood was, "The little wheel's going round."

This short guilt inducing phrase acquired a potency causing all to move into search mode and switch off the offending unnecessary power leak. Such was the efficiency of this short statement none of the children thought to ask just what it really meant until one early evening my brother having been caught after forgetting to turn off the radio-gram, asked innocently," Dad, what is the little wheel?" For a few seconds he paused but quickly regained his authoritive composure and asked us to follow him into the pantry where high up on the white washed wall was the shiny black meter box. Deftly he opened the metallic door revealing a line of fuses, red blinking pilot lights and a small reel of spare fuse wire. Underneath this array of what seemed to us a complex mystery was a separate gadget containing a horizontal shining disc. The little wheel! My father explained that the speed at which it revolved actually measured the amount of electricity being consumed and magically converted it into pounds, shillings and pence before finally becoming the bill (delivered through our letter box) in a brown envelope marked Yorkshire electricity board. Although the little wheel mystery was solved, even to day, 80 years later it is so ingrained in our memories it still evokes a tinge of guilt that somewhere, someone is wasting electricity. "The little wheel's going round!"

# UNCLE MAC AND FRIENDS

The wireless or radio was an important addition to life and an a constant source of information, news and entertainment for the whole family We had a large wooden console with a heavy lid, usually kept closed when not in use in order "to keep the dust off" When open there was a large central tuning knob and a dial for fine tuning to strange names like Hilversum, Munich or Vienna but when the dial was switched to them the only sound was an irritating crackle.

Nearer the front of the set were three smaller knobs. One was for on/off that also controlled the volume; another had three indented colours embossed on it. Green up for medium wave, red up for long wave and white up enabled the use of a 78-RPM gramophone. Skilled manipulation of these dials and knobs enabled us to choose between the Light program, the BBC Home service and the third program – that my father deemed as "too posh" for us with it's fancy music, poetry and plays.

Switching on this piece of "modern technology" it would hum for a few seconds as the valves glowed and warmed up and the dim background light confirmed that it was on.

# Hello Children, Hello Children Everywhere!

Daily, at five o'clock on BBC Home service was Children's hour with an assortment of stories, singing, riddles, puzzles, tongue twisters, humorous tales and news. In an attempt to humanize the presentation a couple of the presenters adopted familial names – the one I recall clearly was Uncle Mac who had a regular feature called, "Larry the Lamb," consisting of fictitious stories about a baby sheep that would loose It's mother or trap it's head in a fence. Even as a child I found his attempts to talk in a quavering "Ba Ba" sheep simulated voice banal and totally unrealistic!

The program finished with the presenter saying," Good-bye children, good bye children every where! Then as a finale for some unfathomable reason the last verse of "On lklely Moor Baht 'tat was played by a brass band. I never really warmed to the "mushy' yet well intended condescending" listen with mother" style and at times could have handed Larry the Lamb over to Hitler and would hasten out side to play cricket in the road.

# CRICKET, CRICKET, CRICKET!

My father made my first cricket bat out of an old plank of wood with the usual markings at the base of the handle being penciled in giving it an authentic appearance. The pitch was the length of the drive but also included the width of the pavement, whilst the wickets were clearly marked in white chalk on the large wooden gates. After ensuring that no cars were coming up or down the road the bowler would run up to the crease (the edge of the pavement) and make his delivery. Conventional rules were rigorously applied except it was only one batsman at a time. If the ball reached the opposite side of the road without bouncing that was six runs but only four if it travelled on the road surface. If the ball ended up in a neighbors garden that was definitely OUT. The presence of cricket at the Spencer's' house was a magnet as within a few minutes five or six little boys (and some slightly bigger ones) appeared from nowhere!

Sometimes my father (a Lancashire cricket addict whose idol Was Cyril Washbrook) would arrive home from work on his James Autocycle demanding that he "Give him a few twisters". So, off came his jacket, and with sleeves rolled up revealing the underlying shiny waistcoat he took the fuzzy tennis ball and became part of the game until my mother opened the large wooden gate and ordered him in.

# A LOVELY BOMB

My father, who was manager of the Sheffield and Ecclesall Co-op pharmacy department had many friends with whom he would "exchange". Toiletries, nappies, soap tonic wine, vitamin pills and other common goods for socks, shoes, spam and other daily commodities.

One of these friends was a smartly dressed character from the clothing department, with what we thought, to be a strange name; Mr Gellsthorpe. How much of these exchange were legal and above board we never asked as it was of obvious mutual convenience!

My memory of Gellsthorp is vague but one day he invited us all for a drive in his new Austin to the seaside. The leather seats seemed luxurious, smelling of opulence and wealth. Gellsthorpe was a cheerful extroverted man and he kept us amused and entertained by his ongoing commentary as we sped through places like Selby, York, Pickering, and the North Yorkshire Moors and on to the seaside town of Filey.

In 1945 Filey bristled with barbed wire defenses, concrete pill boxes, army vehicles, anti-aircraft guns and military personnel. It then became obvious why Gellsthorpe had chosen Filey on the Yorkshire coast, for a day out.

Sitting on the beach was a large mysterious iron sphere at least six foot in diameter with large metal rods sticking out on its surface, reminding one of a prehistoric, highly magnified Corona19 virus. I was desperate to touch it and somehow interact with this strange unearthly metal capsule but was prevented by a barbed wire fence and a large red notice that simply read, DANGER! What was it? where was it from? Were the any extra-terrestrials inside?

My young mind went into fantasy overdrive! What was it? Were there people inside and if so how could they get out? Had it come from outer space in a similar fashion to those little green aliens I had seen in glossy comics?

Whatever its purpose it was a popular distraction from the miserable ponies, sand castles and buckets and spades that characterized this draughty little sea side town.

Gellsthorpe, who seemed to have a broad knowledge of most things explained that the mystery object was an unexploded German mine that had washed ashore at high tide. Fortunately the bomb disposal experts had de-activated it and it was no longer a hazard to citizens and visitors.

This year we are celebrating the 75th anniversary of that terrible war and I still marvel that our childhood experiences were somehow immune to the horrors and miseries enabling us to not only dissociate from it but actually find it a source of fun and excitement.

Historically wars are caused either by territorial disputes or by men seeking fame, revenge, power or elements of all three. Napoleon, Hitler, Pol Pot Mussolini, Stalin, Alexander the Great are just a few that come immediately to mind. I have no urge to discuss the personal psychology of these people as it has already been done and by more competent people than me. What I do find intriguing and remarkable is that whilst we as children were finding the war entertaining and at times fun our parents somehow stoically and courageously kept up brave faces despite knowing what alternatives and horrors could have befallen us all. How did they do it?

The war officially ended on September the first 1945. However, strange as it may seem I have no memory of the event or any ecstatic celebrations that ensued. Life went on as usual. We still played cricket in the drive. We still marched into school, we still had ration books, bananas were still unavailable and Children's hour (including Larry the lamb) was still a feature of the late afternoon. I vaguely recall the reassuring voice of Winston Churchill on the wireless but that was not a new event as I was already familiar with his raspy reassuring voice emanating from our large polished wooden radiogram and even today when I hear recordings of his voice I experience uninvited sensations of nostalgia, moistening of the eyes and a slight bristling of the hairs on the back of my neck.

Thank goodness we won!

Printed in Australia
AUHW011000140622
364939AU00001B/1